BOOK ANALYSIS

Written by Martine Petrini-Poli
Translated by Ciaran Traynor

AF131401

The Myth of Sisyphus

BY ALBERT CAMUS

Bright
≡Summaries.com

ALBERT CAMUS

FRENCH WRITER AND PHILOSOPHER

- **Born in Mondovi (now Dréan), Algeria in 1913.**
- **Died in Villeblevin (France) in 1960.**
- **Notable works**:
  - *The Stranger* (1942), novel
  - *Caligula* (1945), play
  - *The Plague* (1947), novel

Albert Camus was born in French Algeria. He never met his father and spent his childhood with his mother in Algiers. Although his health problems considerably complicated his studies at university (he suffered from tuberculosis), he still managed to obtain a degree in philosophy. He then began a career in political journalism (he joined the Communist Party and started working for the daily newspaper Alger républicain), before leaving for Paris. When the Second World War (1939-1945) broke out, he joined the Resistance movement in Paris and met Jean-Paul Sartre (French writer and philosopher, 1905-1980), who he became friends with. After the Liberation, he became editor-in-chief of the Resistance newspaper *Combat*, where Sartre also worked.

Throughout his life, Camus developed an existentialist philosophy of the absurd, resulting from the awareness that life lacks meaning. He took full advantage of his talents as a writer to spread his philosophy through books, essays and plays. Generally admired and occasionally criticised, Camus' ideas resonated across the world after the release of works like *The Stranger* and *The Plague*.

He received the Nobel Prize in 1957 "for his important literary production, which with clear-sighted earnestness illuminates the problems of the human conscience in our times" (Swedish Academy). He died three years later in a car accident.

THE MYTH OF SISYPHUS

AN ESSAY ON THE ABSURD

- **Genre**: essay
- **Reference edition**: Camus, A. (1955) *The Myth of Sisyphus: And Other Essays*. Trans. O' Brien, J. New York: Vintage Books.
- **1st edition**: 1942 (first English translation appeared in 1955)
- **Themes**: existentialism, the absurd man, suicide, the meaning of life, mythology

The Myth of Sisyphus is an essay on the absurd. It is a part of Camus' cycle of the absurd, which came before his cycle of revolt, along with the novel *The Stranger* and the plays *Caligula* and *The Misunderstanding*.

The Myth of Sisyphus suggests that suicide becomes a consideration when man realises the absurdity of the world, which is to say that existence is devoid of all meaning. According to Camus, although it would not solve the problem, suicide would put an end to man's struggle with the world. It is precisely in the meaninglessness of the world that the meaning of our existence can be found.

Sisyphus, the Greek mythological hero condemned to roll a boulder up a mountain which constantly rolls back down again, is the very image of the human condition for Camus. According to the writer, man must face this destiny with dignity, because he can live happily in the absurd if he does so in full conscience of it.

SUMMARY

"But one day the "why" arises and everything begins in that weariness tinged with amazement" (p. 13). Camus explains that at that moment, the individual becomes aware of the passing of time, the strangeness of the world, its primitive hostility and also the mechanical nature of his actions: he notices that the whole world lives without being aware of death. On an intellectual level, man notices that he is completely sceptical of his knowledge the world and of himself. He therefore begins to wonder if "whether life is or is not worth living" (p. 3).

While he mulls over the meaningless of existence and the futility of everyday human life, Camus comes to define the absurd: it is man being denied "the memory of a lost home or the hope of a promised land" (p. 6). Through this biblical metaphor, he implies that it is as if man has been exiled from his own homeland, from a lost paradise: he is a stranger to his surroundings. The absurd therefore refers to the sense of foreignness man feels towards the world he lives in. But should he escape the absurdity of life with hope or suicide?

The author then analyses a series of existentialist philosophies which attack reason and focus on a religious way of thinking, such as those of Søren Kierkegaard (1813-1855), Edmund Husserl (1859-1938), Lev Shestov (1866-1938), Karl Jaspers (1883-1969) and Martin Heidegger (1889-1976). The author considers that they start off in the right direction, but then end with what he calls philosophical suicide, by which he means escaping towards religion. For the existentialist philosopher Shestov, for example, although reason is pointless, there is something beyond it: he therefore advocates making a leap into the irrational. Camus, on the other hand, refuses to accept this line of thinking and appeal to a God who could only exist by negating human reason.

From Camus' point of view, searching for a meaning to existence beyond the human condition leaves man incapable of understanding freedom, since freedom would be given to him by a higher being. Rather than turning towards religion, he advocates revolt. By revolt, Camus means maintaining the split between the world and the human mind by being constantly aware of the fact that we live in the absurd. It is the only coherent philosophical position. This constant presence of man before himself, this constant consciousness, therefore makes suicide impossible. Faced with suicide, man learns that there is no tomorrow and he is free. In this way, the absurd makes him experience as much as he can, all the while teaching him that all experiences are pointless: they are all equally as important, since none of them have meaning.

There are three consequences to the absurd: passion, freedom and revolt. Camus therefore favours three attitudes which illustrate his recommended way of living:

- **Don Juanism**. Don Juan did not believe in any profound meaning to things: he knew that love is both unique and fleeting.
- **Drama**. An actor lives in the present and can change themselves. Thanks to their roles, they can embody several characters. They are destined to be scattered, since

they have chosen "everywhere" rather than "always" and eternity.

- **Conquest**. The conqueror or the adventurer knows that action in itself is useless. Indeed, nothing lasts in a conquest because, at the end, there is always death; Prometheus, who warred with the gods, was the first modern conqueror: "Yes, man is his own end. And he is his only end. If he aims to be something, it is in this life" (p. 88).

The lover, the actor and the adventurer play the role of the absurd: they are aware of it and live it in complete consciousness of this fact. The creator (the artist) is, however, the most absurd of the characters.

Creating a work is, in Camus' opinion, a unique chance to maintain one's consciousness of the universe. The pinnacle of absurdist joy is therefore creation. It is the "great mime" (p. 94), the "excessive mime under the mask of the absurd". However, the creation of fiction can create the same ambiguities as certain philosophies and escape into the irrational. The real work of art can therefore always be measured by humans, it does not aim to be eternal. Creation teaches patience and clear-sightedness. In fact, man's stubborn revolt against his condition and his perseverance in a futile pursuit is testimony to his dignity.

Kirilov, the hero of the novel *Demons* (1871) by Dostoyevsky (Russian novelist, 1821-1881), believes that he himself is a god if God does not exist, which means that he is completely free on the Earth. If this "metaphysical crime" (p. 108) is enough to fulfil man, why add suicide, Camus asks. In fact, Kirilov wants to show men the way. In Camus' opinion, Dostoyevsky's text touches on the absurd, but is still not an absurdist work since the Russian author provides the reader with an answer.

Campus views Sisyphus as the model absurdist hero: "Sisyphus returning toward his rock, in that slight pivoting he contemplates that series of unrelated actions which becomes his fate, created by him, combined under his memory's eye and soon sealed by his death [...] One must imagine Sisyphus happy" (p. 123).

SISYPHUS, THE MYTHOLOGICAL CHARACTER

"And I saw Sisyphus too, bound to his own torture, grappling his monstrous boulder with both arms working, heaving, hands struggling, legs driving, he kept on thrusting the rock uphill towards the brink, but just as it teetered, set to topple over – time and again the immense weight of the thing would wheel it back and the ruthless boulder would bound and tumble down to the plain again – so once again he would heave, would struggle to thrust it up, sweat drenching his body, dust swirling above his head" (Homer, The Odyssey, p. 269).

This is how Homer (5th century BC Greek poet), describes Sisyphus, the son of King Aeolus of Thessaly and Enarete. He had four children with the nymph Merope. Sisyphus founded Ephyra (now Corinth) and organised the first Isthmian Games, named after the Isthmus of Corinth. He is known for being cunning and deceitful, but is most famous for the punishment reserved for him by the gods after his death.

One day, when he was at the top of the watchtower of the citadel of Corinth, Sisyphus witnessed the kidnapping of the nymph Aegina by Zeus. When the river god Asopus, her father, comes to Corinth to find her, Sisyphus tells him what he saw. Later, after Zeus has escaped Asopus' wrath, the king of the gods sends Sisyphus to Hades, the god of the underworld, to punish him. Thanotos, the personification of death, tries to binds Sisyphus' hands with chains, but Sisyphus claims that they are broken. Sisyphus then tries them on Thanatos, who, discovering himself trapped, realises that the chains work perfectly. The dead take advantage of the situation and escape from the underworld, which the gods soon realise. Ares, the god of war, is charged with setting Thanatos free and delivering Sisyphus to Hades. When he is captured, Sisyphus orders his wife not to offer him the usual offerings the dead receive before leaving for the afterlife. While in the underworld, Sisyphus manages to convince the gods that he must return to Earth to punish his wife, as she has not prepared his burial site, and that he will return as soon as this is done. The plan works, and Sisyphus does not return. The gods therefore await his death to punish him. Guilty of having offended the gods, he is brought to Tartare, in the underworld, where he is condemned to roll a huge boulder to the top of a mountain. However, the boulder continues to fall back down before ever reaching the top, forcing Sisyphus to roll it for all eternity (Schmidt 1983, p. 252).

CONTEXT

In the preface to *The Myth of Sisyphus*, Camus wrote "It is therefore simply fair to point out, at the outset, what these pages owe to certain contemporary thinkers" (p. 2).

Indeed, in the first part of the essay, entitled "An Absurd Reasoning" the author mentions several contemporary philosophers who have strayed from reason. Although Camus always denied being a philosopher, he still remembers something from each concept:

- Heidegger sees man as thrown into existence and living in worry and anxiety, because he is aware of death. This awareness is the very voice of anxiety and implores existence to "return from its loss in the anonymous They" (p. 24).
- Jaspers, who despairs of all ontology (the philosophy of existence), tries to find the path that leads to "divine secrets" (p. 25). From his experience of failure and human powerlessness, he becomes convinced "not [of] the absence but [of] the existence of transcendence" (p. 33).
- Shestov proves that the most universal rationalism will end up coming up against the irrationality of human thought. He exalts human revolt against hopelessness as depicted by Shakespeare (English playwright, 1564-1616), Dostoyevsky, Ibsen (Norwegian playwright, 1828-1906) and Nietzsche (German philosopher, 1844-1900). "We

turn toward God only to obtain the impossible. As for the possible, men suffice" (p. 34), Shestov writes. In fact, he sees God as the absurd, as belief in God demands a denial of reason and a leap into the irrational.

- Kierkegaard also lives in the absurd and sacrifices intellect in the process.
- Husserl and other philosophers of phenomenology (philosophers who observe and objectively describe phenomena and how they appear) restore diversity to the world and deny the transcendent power of reason. Thinking means learning to see again by opening yourself up to intuition. Husserl's phenomenology refuses to explain the world, wishing only to be a description of phenomena and real life. In Camus' opinion, this is the triumph of eternal reason, after having abandoned human reason.

These great minds therefore share a denial of human reason and an evasiveness. Camus denounces these existentialist attitudes.

ANALYSIS

WRITING A PHILOSOPHICAL ESSAY

Like Montaigne (French writer, 1533-1592), Camus wishes to mix thought with the flow of real life. Indeed, the essay is a flexible form which involves a sort of personal commentary on one or more themes in which the personality of the author has a strong presence, thereby bringing together literary writing and philosophical reflection.

Camus' essays also have the following characteristics:

- **Stylisation:** "Great style is invisible stylization or rather stylization incarnate" (Camus, *The Rebel*), Camus explains. It is a question of explaining reality in one's own style. Camus' style aims to reach a serious truth that man experiences: in this way, it moves beyond abstract philosophy. The symbolic representation of man in Sisyphus or Prometheus is what the author calls "stylization incarnate", since these classic myths embody an idea which illustrates his point.
- **Dryness**: the sentences are short, the punctuation is strong and the present is used frequently to describe general truths ("Conquerors know that action is in itself useless", p. 87). In addition, the listing of everyday, repetitive actions accentuates the impression of dryness the writing conveys, and at the same time highlights the mechanical, absurd rhythm of human existence: "Rising; streetcar, four hours in the office or the factory, meal, streetcar..." (p. 12).

- **Understated pathos**: the author frequently says "I" ("That is where I stumble and cling", p. 87). The use of the first person singular moves the reader to reflect and meditate on what they have experienced. Through this, Camus is trying to get through to his reader and move his audience, in order to convey a message which concerns everyone. To do this, he also makes use of oppositions, with the repeated use of the conjunction "but", repeats certain words throughout the text (for example, the word "conqueror" is repeated five times in as many pages), and directly addresses the reader ("Don't assume, however, that I take pleasure in it", p. 87), involving them while holding himself back to a certain extent.

THE MYTH OF PROMETHEUS

In Greek mythology, Prometheus (which comes from the Greek word meaning 'forethought') was a titan.

Prometheus and his brother Epimetheus (literally 'afterthinker') were chosen by the gods to share out divine gifts between man and beast. Epimetheus carried out the task himself, giving animals strength, skill and speed. When it was man's turn, there was nothing left to give. Prometheus therefore decided to steal fire and bring it to Earth. He succeeded, and so men, in spite of Zeus' anger, therefore learned the techniques necessary for them to survive and create civilisation.

Prometheus is the protector of men. One day, when sacrificing a cow to the gods, he separated the animal into two parts. On one side he placed the best parts of the animal, covered in offal and skin, and on the other he placed the bones under a layer of appetising fat. He gave Zeus the choice between the two piles, but the king of the gods did not fall for the trick. Furious, he punished Prometheus and brought misfortune down upon humanity in the form of Pandora (the first woman), as vengeance against human beings.

Prometheus was made to suffer a terrible punishment: he was attached to the Caucasus Mountains, naked, and every day an eagle would come and tear out his liver, which would then grow back before being pecked out again.

EXISTENTIALISM

The etymology of the term "existentialism" comes from the word "existence". On a philosophical level, existentialism is a way of thinking which focuses on existence (the fact that a thing or a being exists), in contrast to philosophies which focus on essence (meaning the attributes which constitute the nature of a thing or being independently of its existence).

On a historical and literary level, existentialism is a philosophical movement which grants greater importance to existence than essence. It is often associated with the work of Jean-Paul Sartre. Existentialism was extremely popular in France between 1943 and 1950.

Even though Camus challenges this term (preferring to use

"philosophy of the absurd"), the influence of existentialism can still be seen in his writing. It develops the themes of Emmanuel Mounier (French philosopher, 1905-1950) in his book *Existentialist Philosophies – An Introduction* (1946), in the chapter "The Dramatic Conception of Human Existence", namely the powerlessness of reason, the contingency of being human (man's existence is unnecessary, which is to say that he exists, but could just as easily not have existed); man's fragility, solitude, alienation, and finiteness; the urgency of death and nothingness.

However, care must be taken to distinguish between two types of existentialism: the Christian existentialism of Gabriel Marcel (French philosopher and writer, 1889-1973) or Mounier, and the atheistic existentialism of Sartre. Mounier, who is careful to link existence and truth together, specifies that a "philosophy which is concerned with the human state is always to some extent a philosophy which is concerned with spirituality" (Mounier, p. 113). He ends his essay with a chapter entitled "The Kingdom of Being is in our Midst" in which he shows that transcendence is at the heart of existence: man is constantly moving towards a "super-being" which is inherent to existence. Sartre, on the other hand, develops a vision of man with no mention of transcendence. In his view, there is no individual essence; it is not determined by human nature. Man is first born and comes into existence, and then freely chooses what he wants to be: in this way, man is nothing other than his plan for himself and the whole of his actions and his choices.

Camus, however, starts from the Nietzschean premise of the

death of God, of *Götterdämmerung*, meaning *"the Twilight of the Gods"*: "Sisyphus teaches the higher fidelity that negates the gods and raises rocks" (p. 123). With the use of an image from mythology, Camus introduces a slight change in meaning between the ancient gods and the Christian God; this is where the refusal of hope, which is subtly linked to the expectations of Christianity, comes from. Indeed, if God is dead, then religion is nothing but a form of evasion, an attempt to escape from the absurd – which is impossible.

THE ABSURD MAN

Man, doomed to die with no hope of salvation, discovers his finiteness. His questions have no answers and come up against an indifferent, possibly hostile nature. His time on the earth is limited to his lifetime. He must therefore compensate for this lack of future with the quantity and quality of his experiences. This is why his model is the absurd man who has learned to live in full consciousness of the absurd and for whom time does not exist, dedicated to the brief intensity of the moment in the role of the Don Juan, the actor or the conqueror.

For this man, time stands still, removed from the course of history. The present becomes the most important time of all, because it is the time of multiple experiences. However, this is not simply gratuitous hedonism; it is rather a revolt against the absurdity of fate.

Man shares the fate of the two heroes of Greek mythology Prometheus and Sisyphus, who were sentenced to eternal punishment for having rebelled against the gods. Unlike in the mythological version, Camus sees the absurd gesture of Sisyphus as leading to a certain form of happiness. Indeed, when he becomes aware of his inevitable fate, the hero experiences a certain joy in the knowledge of his lucidity.

> "This universe henceforth without a master seems to him neither sterile nor futile. Each atom of that stone, each mineral flake of that night-filled mountain, in itself forms a world. The struggle itself toward the heights is enough to fill a man's heart. One must imagine Sisyphus happy" (p. 123).

In the same way, Camus advises men to learn to live with the absurd, because it can lead them to happiness.

THE CYCLE OF THE ABSURD

The cycle of the absurd makes up a part of Camus' body of work, and includes the novel *The Stranger*, the essay *The Myth of Sisyphus* and the plays *Caligula* and *The Misunderstanding*. It ponders the question of the absurd and the absence of meaning in life. There are certain common themes between these works. Indeed, the relationship between essay and story is of paramount importance to Camus. In his opinion, a central profound thought is essential for a work of fiction. This link between philosophy and literature is so strong that the two domains therefore have to overlap.

The Stranger and *The Myth of Sisyphus* explore the founda-tions and the consequences of the absurd. The novel does not illustrate the ideas laid out in the essay, but rather uses the experience which is described in it: namely that of the divorce between mortal man and society. Through the main character of *The Stranger*, Camus does indeed evoke the image of the exiled man, a theme which is also present in *The Myth of Sisyphus*. The essay therefore cannot exist without the novel. Sartre likens the two works in 'An Explication of *The Stranger*':

"*The Stranger*, the first to appear, plunges us without comment into the 'climate' of the absurd: the essay then comes and illuminates the landscape. Now, absurdity means divorce, discrepancy. *The Stranger* is therefore to be a novel of discrepancy, divorce and disorientation" (Sartre, An Explication of *The Stranger*, p. 114).

The novel follows the story of Meursault, a young office worker who has just lost his mother. He slowly comes to the conclusion that life has no meaning, that he is just a cog in the great machine of society. He is a man without ambition who is set in his ways. He lets himself be carried along by events and becomes a murderer by accident – he kills a man because he is blinded by the sun. Stunned, he does not understand what is happening to him and does not try to defend himself or even save his own life: he is sentenced to death.

Meursault is similar to the absurd man that Camus depicts in *The Myth of Sisyphus*: he is a stranger to society. He is a man of habit whose typical day fits the description in the essay: "Rising, streetcar, four hours in the office or the fac-tory, meal, streetcar, four hours of work, meal, sleep, and Monday Tuesday Wednesday Thursday Friday and Saturday according to the same rhythm—this path is easily followed most of the time" (p. 12).

Meursault never tries to escape this chain of routine and absurd events, and only wakes up to reality at the end of his life; conversely, the man in *The Myth of Sisyphus* comes to terms with his condition well before he faces death. The accumulation which symbolises his work day (rising, streetcar and so on) comes to an end, in the essay, with a stirring of consciousness: "But one day the "why" arises and everything begins in that weariness tinged with amazement" (p. 13). In his essay, Camus mentions the men who have woken up: the Don Juan, the actor and so on. In a way, he shows the way of thinking and the path to take in order to free oneself of the absurd.

In *The Myth of Sisyphus*, Camus mentions the demand for clarity which man desires in his relationship with the world. Our whole being demands meaning, both in real life and our personal life: "Understanding the world for a man is reducing it to the human, stamping it with his seal" (p. 17). However, this "nostalgia for unity, that appetite for the absolute illustrates the essential impulse of the human drama" (Ibid.), since life itself is absurd. In the same way, in *The Stranger*, the court – as well as the reader – attempts to find the meaning of the crime committed by Meursault and to give his actions some degree of coherence, while Meursault himself is incapable of doing so: apart from the blinding sun, he has no justification. There is no meaning to his action, since life is absurd, but the court is incapable of hearing this reality and therefore attempts, in vain, to find a reason for the murder.

At the end of the trial, Meursault is therefore sentenced to death. This allows him to finally understand and to be at peace with life: it is only in the face of death that he accepts his strangeness and therefore the absurdity of the world. Consequently, he awakens just before dying, unlike the man in *The Myth of Sisyphus*, who comes to terms with his condition as soon as he realises that life is absurd.

The Myth of Sisyphus, in presenting the absurd man, therefore refers back to the story of Meursault in *The Stranger*. However, while Camus in his novel develops the case of the man who does not rebel and submits to the absurd, in his essay he conveys a much more positive message. He wants to show the reader the absurd and the three consequences which it has: revolt, freedom and passion.

REVOLT

At the end of *The Myth of Sisyphus*, Camus sums up the consequences of comprehending the absurd: "Thus I draw from the absurd three consequences, which are my revolt, my freedom and my passion. By the mere activity of consciousness I transform into a rule of life what was an invitation to death – and I refuse suicide" (p. 64).

According to Camus, revolt is the only way of living in an absurd world. He sees Sisyphus as happy because he rebels against divine laws and takes responsibility for his action. In doing so, he frees himself from the gods and becomes free to live the destiny that he chose for himself: he is no longer condemned to carry the rock to the top of the mountain, but chooses to do it, thereby becoming the master of his own destiny. Sisyphus' eternal labour therefore represents the human condition. Each of us is free to choose to suffer it or not.

> "The workman of today works every day in his life at the same tasks, and this fate is no less absurd. But it is tragic only at the rare moments when it becomes conscious. Sisyphus [...] knows the whole extent of his wretched condition: it is what he thinks of during his descent. The lucidity that was to constitute his torture at the same time crowns his victory" (p. 121).

Camus therefore establishes the cause and the foundation of revolt in his essay. *The Myth of Sisyphus* is therefore linked with the cycle of revolt, which is made up of *The Plague* and *The Rebel*. What is more, this final essay can be read as a response to *The Myth of Sisyphus*. In *The Rebel*, Camus develops an idea similar to the one present in his 1942 essay: without revolt, man is not aware of his freedom. In this work, the author begins with the moral objective of revolt and anchors it in the historical context of the time. Man is therefore viewed within the people; he must revolt against slavery in contemporary society. It is therefore a collective rebellion which leads Camus to say "I rebel, therefore we exist" (*The Rebel*, 2000).

Thanks to revolt and the realisation of the absurdity of life, man experiences true freedom, since he sees the world with fresh eyes, in total clarity. It is at this point that we come to the third consequence: passion. "Aware of one's life, one's revolt, one's freedom, and to the maximum, is living, and to the maximum" (p. 63). Indeed, passion increases the number of experiences man can have.

The Myth of Sisyphus therefore plays an important role in Camus' work since it acts as a link between the cycle of the absurd and the cycle of revolt. In order to give physical form to his musings, the author uses the mythical figures of Sisyphus (*The Myth of Sisyphus*) and Prometheus (*The Rebel*). The use of these two characters is not accidental. In *The Myth of Sisyphus*, Sisyphus personifies the absurd man and in *The Rebel* he is used to represent revolt. In fact, Sisyphus and Prometheus embody the two times of revolt: the first, on an individual level, refuses the condition which the gods impose upon him; the second supports the cause of man and incites him to freedom. Sisyphus is therefore a key character who links the absurd with revolt.

Camus therefore takes an ancient myth and adapts it to give it a modern meaning, in line with his own ideas. In fact, the author wishes to open our eyes with his essay, having written it during the Second World War. He explains in a letter in 1939 that: "People say 'It's absurd'. And then they go and pay their taxes or send their daughter to a private religious school. They think that the matter is finished when they say 'it's absurd'. In reality, it is only beginning"[1] (Politis, 2009: p. 225). This one thought gave rise to the entire cycles of the absurd and revolt. Thanks to his philosophy of the absurd, the author wants to help people to become aware of the absurd and therefore achieve freedom: "And what I want to draw from this [premise] is a certain human, clear-sighted way of thinking, a way of thinking limited in time – a certain behaviour where life will be armed for itself and not

---

1. This quotation has been translated by BrightSummaries.com.

for the daydreams it gives pretext for"[2] (Ibid.). In this sense, Camus is a humanist author, in the modern sense of the term, who exalts a morality of solidarity in the face of an unreasonable world.

---

2. This quotation has been translated by BrightSummaries.com.

FURTHER REFLECTION

SOME QUESTIONS TO THINK ABOUT...

- What is the absurd, as Camus sees it?
- In Camus' opinion, what is an "absurd man" and what are the three roles he can take?
- How does the author's writing back up what he says?
- How is The Myth of Sisyphus structured?? Comment on it.
- In your opinion, why did Camus turn to myths for inspiration for this essay?
- Can a parallel be established between the feeling of being an outsider to the world experienced by man, in the works of Camus, with what Roquentin, the main character of Sartre's *Nausea*, feels?
- What is the difference between Camus' revolt and Sartre's revolution?
- Can Camus' revolt be described as a "drama of atheist humanism", as in the title of a book by Henri de Lubac (French Jesuit theologian, 1896-1991)?
- How does *The Myth of Sisyphus* compare to the rest of Camus' works? Which other books by Camus can it be compared with??
- Pascal (French mathematician, physicist and writer, 1623-1662) and Camus acknowledge that the experience of the limit is inseparable from the human condition. Pascal considers misfortune to have come from man's original sin, whereas Camus accepts the contingency, immanence and fragility of life: "The absurd is lucid reason noting its limits." Compare their points of view.

We want to hear from you!
Leave a comment on your online library
and share your favourite books on social media!

FURTHER READING

REFERENCE EDITION

- Camus, A. (1955) *The Myth of Sisyphus: And Other Essays*. Trans. O' Brien, J. New York: Vintage Books.

REFERENCE STUDIES

- Camus, A. (2000) *The Rebel*. Trans. Bower, A. Bungay: Penguin Modern Classics.
- Cruickshank, J. (1998) Albert Camus. *Encyclopedia Britannica*. [Accessed 10 March 2017]. Available from: <https://www.britannica.com/biography/Albert-Camus>.
- The Editors of Encyclopædia Britannica. (1998) Sisyphus. *Encyclopedia Britannica*. [Accessed 10 March 2017]. Available from: <https://www.britannica.com/topic/Sisyphus>.
- Homer. (1996) *The Odyssey*. Trans. Robert Fagles. New York: Viking Penguin.
- Mounier, E. (1948) *Existentialist Philosophies - An Introduction*. Trans. Blow, E. London: Rockliff.
- Politis, H. (2009) Le Mythe de Sisyphe d'Albert Camus, ou l'absurde comme outil de résistance. *Philosopher en France sous l'Occupation : actes des journées d'études organisées à la Sorbonne, 2000-2002*. Paris: Publications de la Sorbonne. p. 225.
- Schmidt, J. (1983) Larousse Greek and Roman Mythology. Trans. O'Halloran, S. New York: McGraw-Hill Education. p. 252.

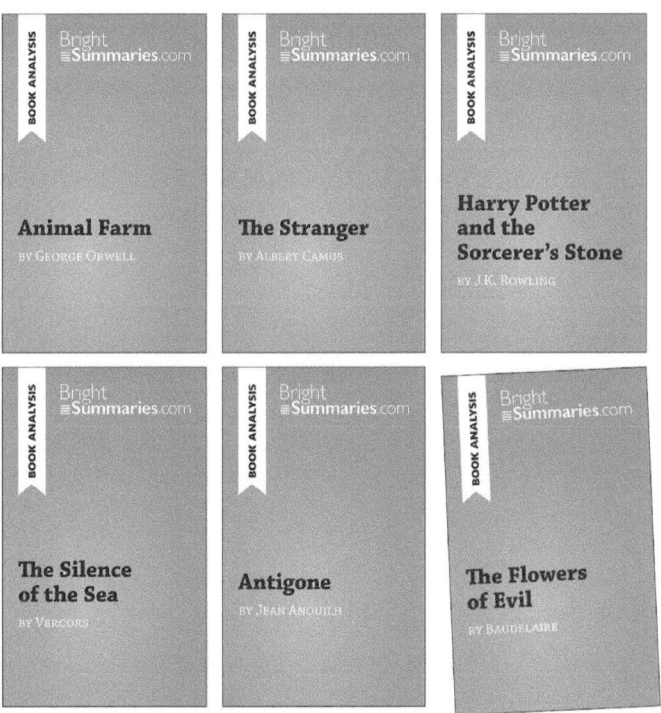

www.brightsummaries.com

Ebook EAN: 9782806294623

Paperback EAN: 9782806294630

Legal Deposit: D/2017/12603/121

This guide was written with the collaboration of Pauline Coullet for the author's biography, the section on the myth of Prometheus and the chapters 'The absurd cycle' and 'Revolt', and the collaboration of Alexandre Randal for the section 'Sisyphus, the mythological character'.

This guide was produced with the support of the *Service Général des Lettres et du Livre of the* Wallonia-Brussels Federation.

Cover: © Primento

Digital conception by Primento, the digital partner of publishers.